The Lord's Prayer:

Accountability and Action

Barry A. Allen

To: Georgia
the good
Keep up
work For Jesus!
I love you!
Rev. Dr. Barry a. allen)
10-14-2017

1

All Scripture references are from the

King James Version of the Bible

For Libby,
My Wife, Companion, Best Friend,
and Fellow Warrior in the
Good Fight of Faith, We Will Love, Serve,
and Fight for Jesus and His Kingdom,
Together Forever

Contents

Chapter 1 – Introduction

Prayer: The Center of Christian Discipleship

The Lord's Prayer is found in the middle of Jesus' great Sermon on the Mount. The Sermon on the Mount in Matthew Chapters 5 through Chapter 7 is our Lord's extensive and detailed teaching on Christian discipleship. In these three chapters in the Gospel of Matthew, Jesus addresses many of the foundational tenets of the Christian Faith and what is required of men and women who choose him as their Lord and Savior. Interestingly, the Lord's Prayer is located in the center of the Sermon of the Mount. This can serve to remind us that prayer is at the center of the Christian Life. As Christians, we are to be people of prayer, Scripture, faith, worship, devotion, evangelism, teaching, and outreach. We are able to do all of these things as the Church when we are people of prayer and the Word. The simple fact that the Lord's Prayer is physically found in the center of the Sermon on the Mount reminds us that we are to keep prayer, communicating with God through speaking and listening, in the middle of our Christian walk with God as we journey through our lives here on earth in the Church Militant.

The Model Prayer

The Lord's Prayer, located in Matthew 6:9-13, is given to us as a model or guide to prayer. We are not "required" to pray it the way it is literally written, but many Christians do. We don't pray it out of duty; we pray it out of love. We love the One who gave the prayer to us. Our Lord Jesus Christ taught his disciples this prayer. However, he was teaching it to them as a model or guide for their prayers. Many of us Methodist Christians pray the Lord's Prayer literally, word for word, every Sunday in our worship services. We don't do this because we are "required" to; we do this for the same reason we follow and obey the more difficult teachings of Jesus like loving enemies and forgiving those who have hurt us. We pray the Lord's Prayer because we want to, and we love the One who gave the Prayer to his disciples, the church, two thousand years ago. We pray this prayer while seeking God's grace and power to live out the Prayer in our daily lives. Many other Christian denominations pray the Lord's Prayer literally, word for word, in their worship services. The Lord's Prayer is a powerful symbol of our unity as Christians in the universal church throughout the world.

A Guide and Source of Christian Accountability

The themes highlighted in the Lord's Prayer also help us to hold ourselves, and others, accountable as Christian disciples. Since it is a model for prayer, it reminds us to not only pray about these important Christian practices, but we are to be doing them as well. As the apostle James states, we are to be "…doers of the word, and not hearers only…" (James 1:22). Jesus concludes the Sermon on the Mount with an important teaching about doing the things he teaches and not just hearing them. In Matthew 7:24-27, Jesus proclaims:

> Therefore whosoever heareth these sayings of mine, and doeth them, I will liken him unto a wise man, which built his house upon a rock:

And the rain descended, and the floods came, and the winds blew, and beat upon that house; and it fell not: for it was founded upon a rock. And every one that heareth these sayings of mine, and doeth them not, shall be likened unto a foolish man, which built his house upon the sand: And the rain descended and the floods came, and the winds blew, and beat upon that house; and it fell: and great was the fall of it.

Talk is indeed cheap, and many claim to love and follow Jesus. However, Jesus makes it very clear throughout the Gospels that those who love him, and live for him, will not only hear his teachings, but they will also do them in their daily lives. They will obey his Great Commandments, and they will love God and love their neighbors including their enemies and strangers. Jesus says we will practice love for God and our fellow man if we really love our Lord when he plainly states: "If ye love me, keep my commandments" (John 14:15).

By praying the Lord's Prayer literally, word for word, and by allowing it to be a guide to prayer and Christian discipleship, we are consistently reminded to keep ourselves in God's will by consistently trusting and obeying the teachings of Jesus. Some of the important aspects of Christian discipleship found in the Lord's Prayer include keeping God first in our lives, reverence for God, growing in holiness as God's kingdom comes in our lives, trusting God to provide our daily physical and spiritual nutrition, receiving and offering forgiveness, resisting sin, and glorifying God and helping in the expansion of his kingdom which is without end. When we are not doing these things in our lives, the Holy Spirit will convict us when we pray the Lord's Prayer in church on Sunday mornings. We will hear that still small voice in our inner selves saying "...repent and return to God."

The Christian who lives in blatant disobedience to his Lord lives in a sort of self-imposed misery, and he or she has no one to blame but him or herself. God does not lead us into temptation, and he never leads us into sin. We choose sin and death when we make decisions with our flesh instead of our Spirits. St. Paul says:

> ...the fruit of the Spirit is love, joy, peace, longsuffering, gentleness, goodness, faith, meekness, temperance: against such there is no law. And they that are Christ's have crucified

the flesh with the affections and lusts. If we live in the Spirit, let us also walk in the Spirit. (Galatians 5:22-25)

Paul also declares "…Walk in the Spirit, and ye shall not fulfil the lust of the flesh" (Galatians 5:16). As Christians, who have the Holy Spirit within and around us, we always have the opportunity to say "no" to sin and "yes" to obedience and holiness. We have a choice. Do we love Jesus enough to obey his teachings, even when it involves loving our enemies and forgiving those who have mistreated us or someone we love? Are we "walking," moving forward in the Spirit through trust and obedience, or are we standing still in the same place we were three, four, or ten years ago. The Lord's Prayer is to be prayed in church Sunday morning, and we will once again be standing in front of our Savior who teaches us to love as we have been loved and to forgive as we have been forgiven. This two thousand year old Prayer, which Jesus taught his disciples, continues to be a guiding light as well as a source of accountability for those of us who call ourselves Christians and strive to live for Jesus in the contemporary world.

The Lord's Prayer and the Unity of the Church

When we Christians pray the Lord's Prayer together in worship services, at funerals and gravesides, and in other ecumenical settings, the Lord's Prayer is a testament to the world, and those around us, of the unity of the Christian Church. Although our Roman Catholic friends shorten it a bit, and our Pentecostal and Church of God friends frequently refrain from praying it together in worship, word for word, due to concerns about repetition and formality possibly quenching the movement of the Spirit, we nevertheless all agree in the importance of the Lord's Prayer and the themes communicated by Christ within it. When we pray it, alone or with other Christians, we are reminded that we have found and dedicated ourselves and our lives to a community that is larger and greater than any one of us, and we are living our lives for the One who loves us so much "...in that, while we were yet sinners, Christ died for us" (Romans 5:8).

Many have highlighted that Jesus teaches us to pray this way, so the Lord's Prayer might be better referred to as the

Christian's Prayer, or the Disciple's Prayer, or something along these lines. This author encourages exercising caution when one thinks he or she is so theologically astute that it is time to be renaming things the Church has already named for hundreds of years. Certainly, Jesus doesn't need to pray for forgiveness of sins because we know that he "…was in all points tempted like as we are, yet without sin" (Hebrews 4:15). However, Jesus came to the earth to teach and show us how to be the people of God, and one of the great things he left us is the Lord's Prayer.

In this magnificent Prayer given to us by Christ himself, Jesus teaches us to keep God first in our lives, and he teaches us to forgive each other in order to maintain the unity of the church. He teaches us to choose holiness and obedience when we face temptation so that the kingdom of heaven can come to our lives to the glory of God the Father. This is the Lord's Prayer because the Lord teaches us, and showed us, how to make the realities for which we pray in the Prayer to be manifested in our lives here in our individual lives as

Christians and in the unity of the Church throughout the world. Yes, the Lord's Prayer belongs to the Church and to each of us as individual Christian disciples, but it is appropriately referred to as the Lord's Prayer because our Lord, out of his grace and love for humanity, gave us these beautiful and majestic words in the center of his glorious Sermon on the Mount. By coming to earth, bleeding and dying a brutal death on the cross for the forgiveness of us sinners, and rising again on the Third Day so that we who trust in him can become New Creations and live abundant and eternal lives in his kingdom, Jesus taught and demonstrated for us how to live as his disciples. We should hold ourselves consistently accountable to Christ, his Sermon on the Mount, and the important teachings highlighted and emphasized within this great Prayer that he gave us which is appropriately called the Lord's Prayer.

9. After this manner therefore pray ye: Our Father which art in heaven, Hallowed be thy name.

As we begin our exposition of the Lord's Prayer, it is not to be overlooked that the very first word of the Prayer is "our." The Christian life is not lived in a vacuum or in isolation, but it is lived out within a glorious community called the Church. When we accept Christ as our Lord and Savior, we are united in the Spirit with all other born-again Christians throughout the world and even those in heaven! We are no longer alone, but we have become part of this beautiful family we call the Christian Church.

The Unity of the Invisible Church

Those who accept Christ as Savior but are never Baptized and confirmed are part of what we call the Invisible Church. The Invisible Church is made up of all born-again believers who have accepted Christ as Lord and trusted in his broken body and shed bleed at the cross as the only payment for their sins. Those who are never Baptized and confirmed never become members of the Visible Church, but they are saved. Those who accept Christ as Lord and Savior and are Baptized and confirmed become members of the Visible Church here on earth, and they are united to all the others who are saved, Baptized, and confirmed. Unfortunately, there will be some who are members of the Visible Church who have been Baptized and confirmed but have never been saved, and they are part of the Visible Church but are not part of the Invisible Church. Only those who are born-again will be united to the true family that is the church here on earth and in heaven, and Jesus makes this very clear in John 3:3 where he proclaims: "...Verily, verily, I say unto thee, Except a man be born again, he cannot see the kingdom of God."

The Great Commandments: Love and Unity

There are over six hundred laws in the Pentateuch, the first five books of the Old Testament, that God gave to his people to obey in order to have close fellowship with him and with one another. However, when Jesus came and died on the cross, he established the New Covenant so that we are now under grace instead of being under the Law. Nevertheless, the Ten Commandments, and the more than six hundred other laws in the Pentateuch, still stand and are still important. Those who strive for holiness and growth in sanctifying grace will continue to study them, meditate on them, read them, and, when we speak of the Ten Commandments, we will strive, work, desire, and continue to be determined to obey them. We do this, not because we fear getting in trouble with God, but because we love God, and we are living lives of gratitude because of what God has done for us in and through the cross of his Son our Lord, Jesus Christ. The author of Hebrews explains by asserting:

> But Christ being come an high priest of good things to come, by a greater and more perfect tabernacle, not made with hands, that is to say not of this building: Neither by the blood of goats and calves, but by his own blood he entered in once into the holy place, having obtained eternal redemption for us. For if the blood of bulls and of goats, and the ashes of an heifer sprinkling the unclean, sanctifieth to the purifying of the flesh; How much more shall the blood of Christ, who through the eternal

Spirit offered himself without spot to God, purge your conscience from dead works to serve the living God?
(Hebrews 9:11-14)

Because of the blood of Christ shed at the cross, we are under the New Covenant, and we are under grace not law. Nevertheless, there is one law in Christianity, and it is love. In Matthew 22:34-40, a Pharisee attempted to confuse and embarrass Jesus by asking him "...which is the great commandment in the law?" (Matthew 22:36) Jesus responds by proclaiming:

...Thou shalt love the Lord thy God with all thy heart, and with all thy soul, and with all thy mind. This is the first and great commandment. And the second is like unto it, Thou shalt love thy neighbor as thyself. On these two commandments hang all the law and the prophets.
(Matthew 22:37-40)

Here, Jesus plainly states that we obey all of the Law and the Prophets by loving God and loving each other. Christian obedience is not complicated. On the contrary, it is quite simple. If one truly loves God, and truly recognizes what Christ has accomplished for him or her at the cross, he or she will demonstrate that recognition and appreciation by outwardly and overtly loving God and loving, forgiving, serving, helping, and caring for his or her neighbors. Those who refuse to love others, and refuse to forgive others, are either very early in their walk with the Lord or are not really walking with the Lord at all.

Unforgiveness, resentment, holding grudges, racism, prejudice, and a lack of recognition of another Christian's place within the family of God and the Church, tears at the unity of the Church and negatively affects the Church's witness in the world. The very first word of the Lord's Prayer is "our," and we are to be united in our Baptisms and our faith. We are to love and forgive each other, recognizing our human frailty, when we have misunderstandings or when a fellow Christian sins against us. We do this because this is what God has done for each of us through the broken body and shed blood of Christ. Our unity is so important to Jesus that he prayed for it on the night before he went to cross for us by praying:

Neither pray I for these alone, but for them also which shall believe on me through their word; That they all may be one; as thou, Father, art in me, and I in thee, that they also may be one in us: that the world may believe that thou hast sent me. And the glory which thou gavest me I have given them; that they may be one, even as we are one: I in them, and thou in me, that they may be made perfect in one; and that the world may know that thou hast sent me, and has loved them, as thou hast loved me.
(John 17:20-23)

Here, Jesus makes it very clear that he wants us Christians to be united, and he points out that the world will know that God sent him when they observe our unity. Our unity and the "our" of the first word of the Lord's Prayer is preserved when we love, forgive, and care for one another.

If Jesus is truly Lord in our lives, we no longer have the right to hold a grudge or refuse to forgive a wrong done to us by a brother or sister in Christ. Jesus makes the rules in our lives because he is the One who died on the cross to free us from rules. If we truly love him, and have even a rudimentary understanding of the great sin-debt he paid for us at the cross, we will shutter at the idea of disrupting the unity of the Church, by refusing to forgive our brother or sister in Christ, and we will love as we have been loved and forgive as we have been forgiven. Jesus makes it very clear that our unity, which is kept in place by our love, is the definitive sign to the world that we are his disciples as he declares:

> A new commandment I give unto you, That ye love one another; as I have loved you, that ye also love one another. By this shall all men know that ye are my disciples, if ye have love one to another.
> (John 13:34-35)

The Fatherhood of God:
Salvation, Reverence, and Obedience

The second word in the Lord's Prayer is "Father," and this makes the first phrase in the Lord's Prayer "...Our Father..." (Matthew 6:9). Indeed, this magnificent phrase brings into focus much of what the rest of the Lord's Prayer is about, and it also captures in a sense much of what our Lord taught, demonstrated, and made possible for us through his life, ministry, death, and resurrection. Because of what Christ accomplished for us at the cross, we are now able to be God's children, and God is our Father. We are no longer far away from God because of our sins, and we no longer have to go out and get animals such as bulls, goats, pigeons, etc...to present to the priest, so he can sacrifice them to cover and atone for our sins. Instead, we only need to accept Jesus Christ as our Savior, recognizing what his broken body and shed blood accomplished for us at the cross, and also accept him as our Lord, repenting of our sins and turning toward God in faith and obedience.

When individuals accept Christ as their Lord and Savior, they are instantaneously regenerated. This is the New Birth, and they are instantaneously born-again as the Holy Spirit, the Comforter Jesus promised, (See John 14:25-26) comes to dwell within them. The best way to understand regeneration is to recognize the profound change that takes place when the Holy Spirit, the Third Person of the Holy Trinity, comes into a person's life. This changes things forever, and this change is permanent. The person is not completely holy yet, but the beginning stages of holiness are in place as the Holy Spirit begins to move within the individual's heart and soul. The new believer has a level of holiness within them now, even though it may in some cases be a very small level, and he or she has begun his or her glorious journey toward sanctification, with God as his or her Father, and with other Christians as his or her sisters and brothers, in the Family of God we call the Church. .

These new believers are also instantaneously justified in that the blood of Christ is applied to their sins, and they are declared "not guilty" of their sins. They are not "actually" not guilty, but they have been "declared" not guilty by the Judge who now is also their heavenly Father. In a sense, all of this is summed up in the very first phrase of the Lord's Prayer: "...Our Father..." (Matthew 6:9). Because of the blood of Jesus shed at Calvary, we are no longer separated from God due to our sins, but the perfect blood of Christ has permanently atoned for all of our sins. Our Judge has become our Father, and our friend, and we can now walk and talk with him just like Adam and Eve did in the Garden of Eden. However, we cannot think that we can walk and talk with God alone, just us and God, because this is not how it is. Many others have trusted in Christ as Savior and repented of their sins and made commitments to follow and obey Jesus as Lord. We walk with all of them also, and they are our sisters and brothers in Christ. These brothers and sisters come from all walks of life, nationalities, ethnicities, races, various professions, different segments of society, prisoners, criminals, converts from other religions, and so on. This first phrase of the Lord's Prayer reminds us to accept all of them as our brothers and sisters in Christ as we celebrate their conversions with God.

In Luke 15:3-7, Jesus gives us the Parable of the Lost Sheep. He asks those around him, if they had a hundred sheep and one was lost, wouldn't they leave the ninety-nine sheep, and go find the one that was lost? The joy God has when an individual gets saved is apparent in the Parable as Jesus states:

> And when he hath found it, he layeth it on his shoulders, rejoicing. And when he cometh home, he calleth together his friends and neighbours, saying unto them, Rejoice with me; for I have found my sheep which was lost. I say unto you, that likewise joy shall be in heaven over one sinner that repenteth, more than over

ninety and nine just persons, which need no repentance.
(Luke 15:3-7)

Here, we see that our heavenly Father, and the angels, celebrate the conversion of even one sinner. As we grow in holiness, and we consistently obey the Great Commandments by loving God and others, we grow in sanctifying grace, and we become more and more like Jesus. We then begin to understand that other Christians, who may speak a different language than us, or live on the "other side of the tracks," or have different political opinions than us, are actually our brothers and sisters in Christ in this beautiful family, within which we live, that extends around the world and even up to heaven.

We don't ever want to be the cause of discord and dissension within our wonderful family made up of the people of God who accept Jesus as their Lord and Savior. We must always choose forgiveness and love so that the unity of the Church will be maintained, and we can do this because we are now part of the New Creation that God is creating which is the family of God. We are the sons and daughters of God because we have been regenerated since the Holy Spirit came into our hearts and lives at our conversions. This enables and empowers us to make holy and righteous choices such as forgiving things the unconverted would not forgive or loving those the unconverted would not love. As we do this consistently as individuals and as the Church, the world sees that there is something different about us, and they see our Lord, and God is glorified. This is what Jesus speaks of in Matthew 5:14-16 where he declares:

> Ye are the light of the world, A city that is set on a hill cannot be hid. Neither do men light a candle, and put it under a bushel, but on a candlestick; and it giveth light unto all that are in the house. Let your light so shine before men, that they may see your good works, and glorify your Father which is in heaven.

Faith, Reverence, Obedience, and Reward

In Verse 9, after we pray "Our Father," we have the phrase "...which art in heaven,..." (Matthew 6:9). This is an affirmation of faith in God. We pray, as individuals and as the Church, because we believe in God. We believe that God is

27

and that he hears and answers our prayers. Faith is a very important aspect of the religious life, and we Protestant Christians contend that faith is absolutely necessary for salvation. The apostle Paul explains, in Ephesians 2:8-10, where he states:

> For by grace are ye saved through faith; and that not of yourselves; it is the gift of God. Not of works, lest any man should boast. For we are his workmanship, created in Christ Jesus unto good works, which God hath before ordained that we should walk in them.

We pray because we believe, and we believe because we pray. It is a glorious cycle of praying, trusting, obeying, believing, and seeing our prayers answered. The cycle is repeated throughout our journey, we grow holier and closer to God through the gifts of prayer, faith, and obedience.

Although God's grace is always involved, faith and obedience are two of the things that we bring to the table and offer to God. The Scriptures make it very clear that God recognizes and rewards faith and obedience. In 1 Samuel 15:22, we read:

> And Samuel said, Hath the Lord as great
> delight in burnt offerings and sacrifices, as in
> obeying the voice of the Lord? Behold, to obey
> is better than sacrifice, and to hearken than the
> fat of rams.

Here, we see that God recognizes and rewards faith and

obedience. There is an inherent relationship between faith and

obedience, and this is discussed in detail in James 2:14-26.

Yes, we are saved by grace through faith, but faith that saves

will produce good works. We don't obey our Lord's Great

Commandments and do good works in order to be saved, we

obey the Great Commandments and do good works because

we are saved. We are not saved by obedience and good works,

but faith that saves will produce obedience and good works.

And, we don't obey God and do good in order to get him to

love us. We obey God and do good works because we know

that God loved us first and that he continues to love us. The

apostle John sums this up succinctly by stating:

> He that loveth not knoweth not God; for God is
> love. In this was manifested the love of God
> toward us, because that God sent his only
> begotten Son into the world, that we might live
> through him. Herein is love, not that we loved
> God, but that he loved us, and sent his Son to

be the propitiation for our sins. Beloved, if God so loved us, we ought also to love one another. (1 John 4:7-11)

When we pray the Lord's Prayer, this phrase reminds us that there is One who watches, sees, blesses us when we obey, and disciplines and corrects us when we sin. Our lives and sense of purpose and well-being are intricately intertwined with "...Our Father which art in heaven,..." (Matthew 6:9). We believe in God, and we trust God. We understand the magnitude of what Christ has done for us on the cross, and it inspires within us a great love for God and the kingdom of his Son our Lord which is both now and continuously arriving as we trust and obey God by loving our God in heaven who loves us and gave his Son for us so that we might be reconciled unto him. God sees what we do, and he sees what we don't do, and Verse 9 reminds us that he is in heaven watching, rewarding, and withholding rewards as we obey or do not obey him. All of this, salvation to sanctification, begins with faith, and this is highlighted by the author of Hebrews who says "...without faith it is impossible to please [God]: for he that cometh to

God must believe that he is, and that he is a rewarder of them that diligently seek him" (Hebrews 11:6). As Christians, we believe that God is real, and he really gave his very best for us at the cross. We love him, and we want to obey and serve him. We worship Jesus as our Savior, and we obey him as our Lord. This beautiful Prayer that we pray, that came directly from our Lord, helps to remind us who we are and keep us accountable to our Savior who says: "If ye abide in me, and my words abide in you, ye shall ask what ye will, and it shall be done unto you" (John 15:7).

The final phrase of Verse 9 is "...Hallowed be thy name" (Matthew 6:9). Here, Jesus is teaching us to remember in our prayers that we are approaching our heavenly Father who is perfectly holy. This calls for reverence and respect as we approach our Mighty God and Savior. Although prayers can sometimes be fairly informal and sometimes have a conversational tone, we are encouraged in this petition to always keep in mind that God is completely holy and perfect. We are to approach God with the upmost respect and reverence while striving to honor and obey him in both word and deed. As we do this, we have a positive witness in this world, and God, Jesus, and the Holy Spirit "...leadeth [us] in the paths of righteousness for his name's sake" (Psalm 23:3).

Chapter 3 – Matthew 6:10

10. Thy kingdom come. Thy will be done in earth, as it is in heaven.

Here, in the first petition of the Lord's Prayer, Jesus teaches us to pray for the kingdom of God to come, and for God's will to be done, here on earth, in our hearts and lives, as it is done in heaven. As we discuss Verse 10, we will do well to remember what makes the will of God a reality in our lives. Obedience to the Word of God, and the Great Commandments of Christ, make God's will a reality in our lives. We do God's will, and his kingdom comes in our homes, hearts, marriages, families, churches, places of employment, and places of recreation, when we keep our Lord Jesus Christ first in our lives, obeying him as Lord, out of love and appreciation for him as Savior.

In the Gospel of Mark, Jesus begins his earthly ministry by proclaiming: "…The time is fulfilled, and the kingdom of God is at hand: repent ye, and believe the gospel" (Mark 1:15). With the arrival of Jesus, born in a stable and laid in a manger, and wrapped in swaddling clothes, God's mighty movement to redeem men and women to his kingdom began. Along these lines, the apostle Paul says: "...God was in Christ, reconciling the world unto himself,..." (2 Corinthians 5:19). In the birth, life, teaching, ministry, example, death, resurrection, and ascension of the promised Messiah, our Lord Jesus Christ, God came near to us, died for us on a cross, and paved the way for us to accept Jesus as Savior, repent of our sins, and immediately begin living in the kingdom of God. Only the truly converted live in this kingdom, and the only way to be converted is to accept Christ as Lord and Savior. Jesus makes this very clear in John 3:3 where he states: "...Verily, Verily, I say unto thee, Except a man be born again, he cannot see the kingdom of God."

The Kingdom and the Cross

When sinners accept Christ as Lord and Savior, and become born-again Christians, they are united with Christ in his power, glory, resurrection, and victory. At the moment of conversion, sinners are regenerated, as the Holy Spirit comes in to their hearts and lives, and the new Christians are also united to Christ in his humiliation, persecution, suffering, death, and rejection. Theologians refer to this as our "mystical union with Christ." Those who are united to Christ and his Church, through faith and Baptism, will be called to share in and carry his cross.

In Matthew 16:24-25, Jesus explains by asserting: "...If any man will come after me, let him deny himself and take up his cross, and follow me. For whosoever will save his life shall lose it; and whosoever will lose his life for my sake shall find it." Here, Jesus makes it very clear that the joy and happiness of the Christian life is found in sharing in our Savior's suffering and rejection. This world is not our home. We are citizens of another kingdom which is the kingdom of God. The King of our kingdom does not do things the way earthly kings do, and those of us who follow him will obediently do things his way instead of doing things the way men and women of the world do things. We are accountable to the One who taught us to pray this Prayer, and we are to obey the teachings of our King even when we don't understand them or like them.

It is counterintuitive and seems somewhat unwise to love our enemies and to forgive those who mistreat us. However, this is only true when these more difficult aspects of Christian discipleship are viewed from a worldly perspective. Once again, we do not belong to this world nor do we ascribe to its me, myself, and I, "egocentric," or self-centered, approach to life. Because the kingdom of God has come in the coming of Christ, and the New Covenant has been established by his shed blood at the cross, we live in the church age which is the age of grace, and we are no longer under the Law. However, in the kingdom of our Lord and Savior, Jesus Christ, there is one law, and the law of the kingdom of our Savior is love. Jesus explains by asserting:

> These things I command you, that ye love one another. If the world hate you, ye know that it hated me before it hated you. If ye were of the world, the world would love his own: but because ye are not of the world, but I have chosen you out of the world, therefore the world hateth you. Remember the word that I said unto you, The servant is not greater than

his lord. If they have persecuted me, they will also persecute you; if they have kept my saying, they will keep yours also.
(John 15:17-20)

Indeed, many claim Jesus as Lord yet refuse to obey his more difficult teachings. They are content to render only a comfortable amount of obedience to the Savior who endured the most brutal form of capital punishment in the ancient world for them. We want to make sure we are not counted in this number. We don't want to be counted among the large number of "Christians" who celebrate that Jesus is their Savior while refusing to obey him as their Lord. They will miss the glory and joy of true discipleship, and the kingdom will not come in their lives to the degree that it could if they truly and unwaveringly obeyed Christ.

The Kingdom Comes to Those Who Believe and Obey

If we truly believe that Jesus is the Christ, and he died for our sins on the cross, we will obey his teachings. Repentance is a very important part of the salvation process. We are delivered from sins in the here and now as we turn away from and forsake them. Since the born-again believer turns away from and forsakes the sins he or she repents of, God is now in a place where he can truly forgive the sins. Along these lines, St. John proclaims that: "If we confess our sins, he is faithful and just to forgive us our sins, and to cleanse us from all unrighteousness" (1 John 1:9). In other words, God is able to truly cleanse us from sins that we truly repent of and turn away from. If we confess sins to God that we have not also repented of, we will not be able to enter into that peace and joy that true righteousness brings in our lives. If we confess sins to God, but we do not repent of them, we instantly become guilty of them once again the moment we are forgiven. Indeed, this may seem confusing, but it is not. The holiness of the kingdom of God, and the will of God, is done in our hearts and lives, as it is in heaven, when we consistently repent of, and turn away from, our sins and obediently choose God's narrow way which leads to life. Also, if we refuse to obey the more difficult teachings of Jesus, like love for enemies, and forgiving those who have wronged us, we will not see the kingdom here on earth. And, we will not grow more and more like our Savior who teaches us:

> For if ye love them which love you, what reward have ye? Do not even the publicans the same? And if ye salute your brethren only, what do ye more than others? Do not even the publicans so? Be ye therefore perfect, even as your Father which is in heaven is perfect. (Matthew 5:46-48)

Jesus tells us that we are to seek his kingdom first (Matthew 6:33), and he says: "Blessed are they which do hunger and thirst after righteousness; for they shall be filled" (Matthew 5:6). In other words, there is a direct relationship between how much we want the kingdom to come in our lives and how much it actually comes in our lives. If we really love Jesus, and we have even the most elementary understanding of what he accomplished for us at the cross, we will "hunger" and "thirst" for him and his kingdom. As we "hunger" and "thirst" for him, we hold ourselves more and more accountable to his teachings and Great Commandments. As we consistently hold ourselves more and more accountable to the teachings of Christ, our actions begin to reflect repentance of our sins, as we turn away from our sins, and we grow in righteousness and sanctifying grace. This is made possible because of the presence and power of the Holy Spirit in our hearts and lives. The apostle Paul sums this up perfectly by stating:

> ...if ye live after the flesh, ye shall die: but if ye through the Spirit do mortify the deeds of the body, ye shall live. For as many as are led by the Spirit of God; they are the sons of God. (Romans 8:13-14)

I remember when I was a much younger minister, serving my first appointment, right out of seminary, a delightful gentleman in the church told me one day that: "People do about what they want to do." I remember being struck by the simplicity of the statement, and I remember doubting that it was true. As the years have passed, and I am well into what we call "middle age," I have found that, in a free society like we enjoy here in the United States of America, it is indeed true that men and women, for the most part, do what they want to do. This may not be obvious as we see persons consistently making poor choices that lead to sickness, imprisonment, the loss of employment, and the breaking up of their homes and marriages. However, even in these situations, we see that these individuals have consistently chosen drugs and alcohol, materialism, adultery, hatred, animosity, gambling, tobacco, and so on. They decided they wanted to live this lifestyle, and these poor decisions infected and tainted their lives to the point that the quality of their lives was negatively affected.

My parishioner was actually correct. In a free society, people do tend to do about what they want to do. And, the more we want the kingdom of God to come in our hearts and lives, the more we will say "no" to sin and "yes" to righteousness. As we consistently hold ourselves accountable to Christ and his teachings, our actions will be more in line with love for God and neighbor. The result is that we begin doing things the way Jesus teaches us to do them and not the way the world says to do it. Similarly, we begin doing things God's way and not the way our flesh "wants" to do things. As our actions reflect our accountability to what we pray for in the Lord's Prayer, we begin to want things the way God wants them, and we begin to do things the way Jesus does them. This is what true holiness and sanctification look like in our hearts and lives.

Chapter 4 – Matthew 6:11

11. Give us this day our daily bread.

In this petition, Jesus is teaching us to pray for our "daily bread." In other words, we are to ask God to provide for our basic everyday material needs like food, clothes, and shelter. By teaching us to pray this in the Lord's Prayer, Jesus is reminding us that we are completely dependent upon our heavenly Father. Yes, we may work hard, make our money, and buy our food and clothing. However, we are only able to work, make money, and buy food and clothing because of the gifts, talents, and abilities that God has given us. We are completely dependent upon God for our daily physical and spiritual bread. I am frequently amazed, and a little disheartened, when I am out to eat at a restaurant, and I see persons diving into their delicious meals without even saying even a short prayer to God giving thanks for the feast that is before them. As Christians, we know that it is our heavenly Father who provides all of our needs, and he also sometimes provides our wants as well.

Physical and Spiritual Bread

As we follow the model that Jesus gives us in this verse, we are reminded that God provides not only for our physical needs, but he provides for our spiritual needs as well. When Jesus was hungry in the wilderness, and tempted by the enemy to change stones into bread, Jesus declared: "...It is written, Man shall not live by bread alone, but by every word that proceedeth out of the mouth of God" (Matthew 4:4). In other words, we need our spiritual bread just as much as we need our physical bread. If we become physically malnourished, our bodies become weak and vulnerable to sickness and disease. If we become spiritually malnourished, we become spiritually weak and susceptible to temptation, worldliness, selfishness, and pride. When Jesus is tempted by the enemy in the wilderness, we see that he stands upon the spiritual bread of the Word of God instead of on the physical bread of food. (See Matthew 4:1-11 and Luke 4:1-13) By standing on the Word of God, Jesus successfully resists temptation, and the devil departs from him. (See Matthew 4:11 and Luke 4:13)

When we resist the devil, and say "no" to him, he is confronted by the holiness of Christ in us. The devil doesn't like this, and he runs away from the presence and power of the Holy Spirit in us. Along these lines, the apostle James summarily states: "Submit yourselves therefore to God. Resist the devil, and he will flee from you....Humble yourselves in the sight of the Lord, and he shall lift you up" (James 4:7, 10).

God is good, and he provides for our physical and spiritual needs. Does this mean that devout Christians have never starved to death? No it doesn't. Does this mean that devout Christians have never given in to temptation and committed terrible sins? No it doesn't. However, it does mean that God will ultimately provide, in this life or in eternity, for all the physical and spiritual needs of those who have trusted in the broken body and shed blood of Jesus Christ as the only payment for their sins. Indeed, this is what the Psalmist highlights in the first and last verses of Psalm 23 where he proclaims:

> The Lord is my shepherd; I shall not want....Surely goodness and mercy shall

follow me all the days of my life; and I will
dwell in the house of the Lord for ever.
(Psalm 23:1, 6)

In this petition, we are reminded of the importance of asking

God to fulfill not only our physical needs but our spiritual

needs also. We are also reminding ourselves to give thanks to

God for the physical and spiritual nourishment that he

faithfully provides for us. Our physical needs include food,

clothing, shelter, employment, transportation, and other

material things. Our spiritual needs include Scripture, worship,

prayer, fellowship with other Christians, opportunities to

serve, abilities for ministry, healing, forgiveness, the ability to

care and forgive, courage, and strength to answer God's call

on our lives. As we can see, our spiritual needs are just as

important, if not more important, than our physical needs

because it is in providing for our spiritual needs that God helps

us to reach our full potential for his kingdom. This gives us a

great sense of purpose, fulfillment, and joy as the kingdom of

God comes here in our hearts and lives as it is in heaven, and we grow in sanctifying grace and love to be more and more like Jesus who says:

> As the Father hath loved me, so have I loved you: continue ye in my love. If ye keep my commandments, ye shall abide in my love; even as I have kept my Father's commandments, and abide in his love. These things have I spoken unto you, that my joy might remain in you, and that your joy might be full. This is my commandment, That ye love one another, as I have loved you.
> (John 15:9-12)

Faith, the Cross, and the Bread of Life

As Christians, we have faith in God, and we believe that God loves us. Similarly, we believe God loved us so much that he sent his only Son to die for us on the cross. (John 3:16) Therefore, we believe that God will meet our physical needs, and we also believe that God will meet our spiritual needs. We worship and serve Jesus because he is God and Savior, and we celebrate that he met all of our spiritual needs when his body was broken, and his blood was shed, at the cross. This, however, requires faith because we sometimes may "feel" like we are lacking spiritually, and we sometimes may "feel" like we are lacking in the physical realm. We, however, walk and

move forward "...by faith, not by sight..." (2 Corinthians 5:7).
We certainly do not walk, make forward progress, by
analyzing things based on the worldly categories of feeling,
financial gain, and acceptance and popularity in our sinful and
corrupt modern post-Christian culture.

Actually, many in our culture live their lives as if God
doesn't exist, and there is no one to whom they are
accountable or will one day have to answer to for their sinful
and egocentric lifestyles. We Christians, who have chosen the
narrow way that leads to abundant and eternal life in the house
of the Lord, rejoice and celebrate that we no longer live that
way because we love God and what Jesus did for us at the
cross. We don't refrain from sin, and refuse to give in to
temptation, because we are afraid of God's judgment. On the
contrary, we refrain from sin, and refuse to give in to major
temptations, because we love God more than we love this
sinful and fallen world. We love God, and we want his
kingdom to come in our hearts and lives, and we thank God
for what he did for us at the cross incarnate in the Jewish flesh

the our Lord and Savior, Jesus Christ. We celebrate that holiness and the desire to live for and please God has been born in our hearts beginning at the moment of our conversions. We live in the age of grace, and we stand in God's grace. (Romans 5:2) We live for God, and we obey God because we love God. We are thankful to God for sending Jesus to save us, and we want to live lives that bring glory to his name. St. Paul alludes to this in Romans 5:19-21 where he declares:

> For as by one man's disobedience many were made sinners, so by the obedience of one shall many be made righteous. Moreover the law entered, that the offence might abound. But where sin abounded, grace did much more abound: That as sin hath reigned unto death, even so might grace reign through righteousness unto eternal life by Jesus Christ our Lord.

Here, in these powerful verses of Scripture, Paul points out that the disobedience of Adam brought sin and the law into God's creation. Adam's sin also brought death into creation. Because of the sin of this one man, we will all die unless we are alive when the Rapture and Second Coming take place.

And, we can all be righteous by trusting in Christ, and his atoning work at the cross, and by living our lives for Jesus by obeying his Great Commandments by loving God and each other. This brings us abundant and eternal life as we truly trust in Christ as our Savior, repent of our sins, and consistently grow in his righteousness as we grow in sanctifying grace and become more like him. This is the Good News of the Gospel, and the apostle Paul sums it beautifully in 2 Corinthians 5:21 where he proclaims that God "...made him to be sin for us, who knew no sin; that we might be made the righteousness of God in him." In other words, Jesus bore the sins of the world on his shoulders at the cross, and he felt the presence of our sins in his heart and his tattered and torn body. The blood of Jesus bridged the gap that our sin had created between us and God, and we can now walk and talk with God and grow in his grace as righteousness, not sin, reigns in our hearts and lives.

We have all of this by God's grace through faith, and it is God's great gift that is received by trusting in Jesus and his atoning work at the cross. (Ephesians 2:8) The Holy Spirit, the

Third Person of the Holy Trinity, is within and around us, and he leads us "...in the paths of righteousness for [Jesus'] name's sake" (Psalm 23:3).

Jesus is the Bread of Life

In John 6:31-35, we read:

> Our fathers did eat manna in the desert; as it is written, He gave them bread from heaven to eat. Then Jesus said unto them, Verily, verily, I say unto you, Moses gave you not that bread from heaven; but my Father giveth you the true bread from heaven. For the bread of God is he which cometh down from heaven, and giveth life unto the world. Then said they unto him, Lord evermore give us this bread. And Jesus said unto them, I am the bread of life; he that cometh to me shall never hunger; and he that believeth on me shall never thirst.

We Christians are called "Christians" because we believe in Jesus Christ. We believe in what he did, and we believe the things he said. We also believe in living our lives according to his teachings and Commandments. When the born-again believing Christian truly strives to keep Christ first in his or her life and truly tries to live for Jesus day in and day out, he or she will find fulfillment as Jesus provides daily spiritual and physical bread. This doesn't mean the Christian is always on the mountain top because trials and difficulties still come our way from time to time. However, this does mean that the Christian has all things, and can do all things, in and through Jesus Christ. The Psalmist expresses the fulfillment of living a holy life in Psalm 23:5 where he states: "...my cup runneth over." Indeed, the cups of Christians do run over with daily physical and spiritual bread as God answers our prayer that we consistently pray: "Give us this day our daily bread" (Matthew 6:11).

Chapter 5 – Matthew 6:12

12. And forgive us our debts, as we forgive our debtors.

The two most important teachings of Christ are love and forgiveness. In this petition of the Lord's Prayer, we ask God to forgive us of our sins. Although we are growing in sanctifying grace, and through love for God and neighbor we are becoming holier, sin never ceases to be a reality in our lives. However, as born-again Christians, we are no longer slaves of sin. The blood of Jesus has freed us from the power, the penalty, and the presence of sin. It no longer has dominion in our lives, and we are equipped and enabled to say "no" to sin and "yes" to righteousness. The apostle John points this out in 1 John 1:7 where he states: "…if we walk in the light, as he is in the light, we have fellowship one with another, and the blood of Jesus Christ his Son cleanseth us from all sin." We can live in freedom from serious sin if we consistently choose to walk with God in the light. The more we choose obedience instead of disobedience, and the more we say "yes" to righteousness and "no" to sin, the holier we become.

Eventually, God's way becomes our way, and we begin to think and respond to the world in the same way God does. We dislike sin, and we like righteousness. We cherish our life with God, and we refuse to allow anything to get in between us and God. We realize that Jesus Christ is what life is all about, and we come to the glorious realization that we will follow him, and his narrow path of righteousness, to the ends of the earth. By God's amazing grace, we begin to reflect in our earthly lives the commitment and determination of our Savior who said:

> ...I came down from heaven, not to do mine own will, but the will of him that sent me. And this is the Father's will which hath sent me, that of all which he hath given me I should lose nothing, but should raise it up again at the last day. And this is the will of him that sent me, that every one which seeth the Son, and believeth on him, may have everlasting life: and I will raise him up at the last day. (John 6:38-40)

Jesus had great peace, and the fact that he was doing God's will gave him great strength. The obedient born-again Bible reading, praying, and worshipping Christian is a force of hope and holiness that must be reckoned with. He or she is also a great force of love and forgiveness, for these are the most prominent and definitive teachings of Christ.

Praying and Lying to God in Prayer

When we bow our heads in worship on Sunday mornings, and we pray the Lord's Prayer, we ask God to: "...forgive us our trespasses." Then, we tell God, in prayer, that we are forgiving others by praying: "...as we forgive those who trespass against us." Now, prayer is serious business, and even the mildly religious would probably warn against lying to God, in God's house, in prayer, on the Sabbath Day. Yet, this happens very frequently. Christians gather for worship, and pray this petition of The Lord's Prayer, asking God to be merciful and to forgive their trespasses. Then, they tell God they are forgiving those who have trespassed against them, and they ask God to forgive them at the same level that they have forgiven others. This is all good if it is true, and it is only true if the Christian has not closed the door of forgiveness on any other person. If we have made up our minds that we are not going to forgive someone, but we pray this petition of the Lord's Prayer, we lie to God and commit serious sin. We would be better off to just remain silent as the congregation prays: "Forgive us our trespasses, as we forgive those who trespass against us."

The Door and Language of Forgiveness

Forgiving those who have wronged us can be very difficult at times. There are many reasons that sometimes make it very difficult for even us Christians to forgive those who have hurt or mistreated us. It is as if we have written in certain exceptions to the teaching of Jesus in Scripture. Some of the impediments to forgiveness include the gravity of the wrong done to us, the lack of remorse or repentance demonstrated by the offender, a refusal to love and see the offender as a human being, the desire for revenge, and a desire to make the offender "pay" by terminating the relationship which demonstrates that no true forgiveness has taken place. All of these "reasons" are not really reasons but are "excuses" that the so called "Christian" uses in order to retain and indulge in his or her "fleshly" desire for revenge and retaliation. Indeed, may persons who stand up in God's house on Sunday mornings, in front of his altar, and in the presence of his people and affirm by reciting the Apostles' Creed that they believe in Jesus Christ and the forgiveness of sins, occasionally do not demonstrate this belief in their everyday lives as they pick and chooses who they will forgive and who they will love.

In this powerful petition of the Lord's Prayer, we ask God to forgive "all" of our sins, and we tell God that we have, or are actively trying to, forgive "all" of the sins that have been committed against us. We pray this petition with integrity as long as we have not closed the door of forgiveness on any person. We may not have forgiven them completely, but we are still trying to forgive them. Verse 12 can be understood as us praying: "God, please forgive us our sins as we continue to strive and work toward completely forgiving those who have sinned against us." I frequently use the idea that there is a specific "forgiveness" door on the heart of every person. As

Christians, we are prohibited from locking this door, and we are prohibited from closing the door on any person. Yes, I said any person. The Christian is called to love and forgive every person, and this is the way it is in the kingdom of our Lord and Savior, Jesus Christ.

Only Jesus is Lord, and we who worship and follow him must render unto him the obedience that is due him. This obedience is manifested in our lives as we love as he first loved us, and we forgive as he has forgiven us. We don't want to arrive at the Judgment Seat of Christ (2 Corinthians 5:10) and find that Jesus decided to pick and choose which of our sins would be forgiven and which sins would not be forgiven. It would only take one sin, even a relatively minor sin, to keep us separated from God forever. We want to arrive at the Judgment Seat of Christ to receive our rewards, and to have rewards withheld, while not receiving any punishment because "all" of our sins have been covered and atoned for by the blood of Christ. Therefore, if we want "all" of our sins to be forgiven, we must forgive "all" of the sins committed against us by others. The door of forgiveness on our hearts cannot be slammed shut on any persons just as we don't want God to pick and choose only certain sins to be forgiven by the atoning work of Jesus on the cross.

The door of forgiveness on the heart of every person can be likened to a very strong, thick, and reinforced door with at least two locks. This door is "open" in the hearts of truly born-again Christians who have walked with the Lord many years. Forgiveness easily travels from God and others into their hearts, and forgiveness is granted and flows easily out of their hearts to others. Forgiveness is granted quickly, without reservation, because we have decided to honor Christ as Lord and to obey his teachings that we love and forgive others the way he loves and forgives us. The door of forgiveness on the heart of the truly saved and obedient Christian is always open, allowing love and forgiveness to easily flow in and out, as he or she consistently obeys the teachings of Jesus who says:

> Be ye therefore merciful, as your Father also is merciful. Judge not, and ye shall not be judged: condemn not, and ye shall not be condemned: forgive, and ye shall be forgiven: Give, and it

shall be given unto you; good measure, pressed down, and shaken together, and running over, shall men give into your bosom, For with the same measure that ye mete withal it shall be measured to you again.
(Luke 6:36-38)

Here, Jesus points out that mercy and forgiveness are governed by the Law of the Harvest. (See Galatians 6:7-10). The Law of the Harvest is a universal law, like the Law of Gravity, that is in place and affects every person whether they believe in it or not. It is the idea that what we sow, we will reap. If we sow love, mercy, and forgiveness, by loving and forgiving others, love and forgiveness will come back to us. If out of hardness of heart, and the fleshly desire for revenge and retaliation, we judge and without mercy hold others fully accountable for the sins they commit against us, we will be unable to find and receive mercy and forgiveness when we need it. God's forgiveness is there, but the unforgiving, hard-hearted, and disobedient Christian's door of forgiveness on his or her heart is closed. When a door is closed, it is closed from both sides. Forgiveness can't find its way out to others, and forgiveness can't come in from God and others. This should not be the case because Jesus bled and died for us on the cross so that we could be forgiven, and we are to forgive others as God has forgiven us. What we sow, we will reap. If we sow love, mercy, and forgiveness, the door of forgiveness on our hearts will be open to allow the love, mercy, and forgiveness to flow out and into the lives of others. The reality of the Law of the Harvest, as it pertains to forgiveness and mercy, is evident in the Fifth Beatitude where Jesus declares: "Blessed are the merciful; for they shall obtain mercy" (Matthew 5:7). Mercy and forgiveness return to those who offer it to others because the door of forgiveness on their hearts is open, and it allows forgiveness to flow both in and out.

Those "Christians" who have decided to close the door of forgiveness on their hearts to certain persons due to the gravity of the sin they committed, their lack of repentance, or the fleshly desire to retaliate and get even, must remember that when a door is closed, it is closed from both sides. As mercy and forgiveness is unable to flow out to others, the mercy and forgiveness of God and others are unable to flow into the heart also. This hardness of heart causes a breakdown in this "Christian's" relationships with God and others, and he or she becomes more and more isolated from God and others as the sinful desire for retaliation and revenge takes precedence and the teachings of Christ are not honored and obeyed.

Learning to Forgive is like Learning a Foreign Language

I remember vividly when I returned to college in 1992 to begin studying for the ministry. I received Christ as my Lord and Savior in October of 1990, and I began feeling the call to ministry in 1991 and 1992. I returned to college with great trepidation. This time I would not be able to withdraw when the classes got too hard, or I grew weary of reading, taking exams, and writing research papers. I was especially concerned about the English Classes and the Foreign Language Classes. I had made a feeble attempt to go to college back in 1982 after I graduated from High School, but I withdrew because of a general lack of interest and sense of purpose. I remember, however, that the level of difficulty in the Freshman English I was taking was also a contributing factor in my decision to withdraw. Freshman English is oftentimes regarded as a "Weeder Course" in many colleges and universities. In other words, it is thought by many to be one of the courses that helps separate, or "weed out," the unsuccessful students who are not focused, determined, and dedicated to their studies from the students that will succeed and ultimately graduate with the coveted Baccalaureate Degree four years later. This time I made up my mind that I would be counted among the latter, and I would work hard and do what it took to pass Freshman English and the dreaded and required Foreign Language Courses.

I signed up to take French. I remember starting from the beginning, learning vocabulary and how to conjugate verbs, and eventually how to form and speak sentences. It was a long process that required much energy and effort. This is why the college required three semesters, or nine hours, of foreign language, so that we would stay at it long enough for it to sink in. Learning to love our enemies and to forgive those who wrong us is much like learning a foreign language. When we come to Christ, accept him as Lord and Savior, the Holy Spirit comes into our hearts and lives, and we are born-again. As the Holy Spirit moves and works in our hearts and lives, we begin to be convicted of certain sins, and we are strengthened, empowered, and enabled to begin living for God and growing in holiness. Sanctification is a process, and it takes time, discipline, energy, and effort. As we grow in sanctifying grace, we grow in our knowledge and understanding of the teachings and Commandments of Christ. We now regard Christ as Lord and Savior, and his teachings are no longer mere suggestions.

The teachings and Commandments of Christ are the wishes of our Savior. We live according to his teachings because he is Lord and Savior, and we no longer conduct ourselves in the ways of this fallen world. We conduct ourselves in the narrow way of Jesus Christ. Only Jesus is Savior, and only Jesus is Lord, so we strive to obey his teachings and Commandments which require us to love God and love and forgive every person, including our enemies. Like learning a Foreign

Language, we first learn to take small steps in the areas of love and forgiveness. We find ourselves praying for the guy at work who curses and lives a sinful life. Then, as we grow more knowledgeable of the teachings of Jesus, and closer in our relationship to God, we begin holding ourselves accountable to the more challenging teachings of Jesus like loving enemies and forgiving those who mistreat or persecute us. The true joy of Christian discipleship is found in this radical accountability to the "difficult" teachings of Christ because those who obey his most challenging teachings are the ones who truly honor, reverence, and obey him as Lord. Jesus Christ is honored, obeyed, and worshiped as Lord in the life of the Christian disciple who obeys Jesus' teachings that we love enemies and forgive everyone; the Lord's Prayer, especially in Verse 12, offers us guidance and direction, leading to accountability and action, as we strive to obey Jesus as Lord in our daily lives as Christian disciples.

My Dad and I went to Paris, France in the Summer of 1993 after I had completed two semesters of French. We were able to order meals in French and greet people in French. As we rode the bus out to Normandy and Omaha Beaches, we carried on limited but cohesive conversations with one another in French on the bus. Daddy had studied French on his own as a hobby for several years, and I had studied it for a year in college. We were familiar with the language of the country we were in and that, coupled with the fact that my Dad is a World War II Veteran, made us fit right in. If we want to fit in in the kingdom of our Lord and Savior Jesus Christ, we must learn to speak the language of love and forgiveness.

We pray Verse 12 with integrity as long as we are trying to forgive those who have wronged us. It is not hypocritical to pray Verse 12 if we are still trying to forgive the person or persons we have not yet forgiven. Referencing the idea of the forgiveness door of the heart, we are not lying to God if we have unlocked both the lock on the doorknob and the deadbolt. We are not lying to God as long as we are still grabbing the doorknob and trying to open it. We are not lying to God as long as we continue to pray and ask God to gives us the grace we need to forgive the person we still haven't forgiven. As long as we are actively still trying to forgive, we can pray Verse 12 of the Lord's Prayer with integrity and confidence and with hope that God will answer the prayer and eventually we will be able to completely forgive the individual or individuals. However, if we have slammed shut the door of forgiveness on our hearts, and have made the conscious decision to never forgive the person, we pray hypocritically and lie to God in prayer when we pray: "Forgive us our trespasses as we forgive those who trespass against us."

Lying to God in prayer, in God's house, while praying with God's people, on God's Sabbath Day, is probably not wise. Therefore, until the person begins trying to forgive, he or she should probably refrain from praying Verse 12 where Jesus teaches us to pray: "And forgive us our debts, as we forgive our debtors" (Matthew 6:12). If we have learned how to forgive others by learning the language of forgiveness, we will be able to speak the language when we need forgiveness. If we haven't learned the language of forgiveness, by forgiving others and keeping the forgiveness door on our hearts open, we will not be able to speak the language of forgiveness when we need forgiveness. As Christians, we have the Lord's Prayer to help us regularly make sure that we are holding ourselves accountable, and our actions are reflecting that we are holding ourselves accountable, to the teachings of Christ that call upon us to love and forgive everyone. This teaching is evident in Matthew 5:44-48 where our Savior says:

> But I say unto you, Love your enemies, bless them that curse you, do good to them that hate you, and pray for them which despitefully use you, and persecute you; That ye may be the children of your Father which is in heaven: for he maketh his sun to rise on the evil and on the good, and sendeth rain on the just and on the unjust. For if ye love them which love you, what reward have ye? Do not even the publicans the same? And if ye salute your brethren only, what do ye more than others? Do not even the publicans so? Be ye therefore perfect, even as your Father which is in heaven is perfect.

13. And lead us not into temptation, but deliver us from evil:
For thine is the kingdom, and the power, and the glory,
for ever. Amen.

In this petition of the Lord's Prayer, we are basically asking God to help us make the right decisions in our lives, and we are asking him to help us choose the way of holiness instead of the way of sin. The fact that we are praying asking God not to "…lead us into temptation,…" (Matthew 6:13) has been the cause of some confusion and debate. However, this should not be because we know that God never leads anyone into sin, but we sometimes choose sin instead of righteousness. In James 1:13-16, the apostle James explains by asserting:

> Let no man say when he is tempted, I am tempted of God: for God cannot be tempted with evil, neither tempteth he any man: But every man is tempted, when he is drawn away of his own lust, and enticed. Then when lust hath conceived, it bringeth forth sin: and sin, when it is finished, bringeth forth death. Do not err, my beloved brethren.

We always have a choice, and we always have the opportunity to choose obedience instead of disobedience. In Verse 13, we are asking God to help us to make the right choices which keep us in that narrow way of holiness which leads to abundant and eternal life in the kingdom of God. God answers this prayer, and we are empowered and equipped to choose holiness, and to walk in the narrow way of Christ, because of the presence of the Holy Spirit within and around us and by the amazing grace and goodness of our loving God.

God's Faithfulness and Making the Right Choices

Because God is faithful, we always have the option to make the right choice when we are confronted with temptation. If we had no opportunity to choose obedience and holiness, God would not be faithful, and he would not be just. If God led us into temptation, he would be participating in the sin, and we know that God is completely holy and without sin. Sin is something we do, and it is something we choose. God takes no part in it except that he forgives us of it when we repent and turn away from it. This year, in October, I will celebrate the 27th Anniversary of my conversion. I have walked with God, Jesus, and the Holy Spirit for over a quarter of a century, and I can assure you that God is faithful. God's great faithfulness is one of my favorite things about God. God has never abandoned me, and I celebrate the truth proclaimed by Jeremiah in Lamentations 3:21-25 where he states:

> This I recall to my mind, therefore have I hope. It is of the Lord's mercies that we are not consumed, because his compassions fail not. They are new every morning: great is thy faithfulness. The Lord is my portion, saith my soul; therefore will I hope in him. The Lord is good unto them that wait for him, to the soul that seeketh him.

By God's amazing grace, and his presence among us in the person of the Holy Spirit, we are empowered and equipped to choose and walk in obedience and righteousness. Because we always have the option of obedience, sin is always our fault when we choose it.

At the very moment of conversion, the Holy Spirit comes to dwell in the heart and life of the Christian, and he or she begins the journey toward sanctification. He or she now has the Holy Spirit, the very presence of God, in his or her life to help him or her choose the way of obedience and holiness.

Before ascending to his Father, Jesus promised this by stating:

> And I will pray the Father, and he shall give you another Comforter, that he may abide with you forever; Even the Spirit of truth; whom the world cannot receive, because it seeth him not, neither knoweth him: but ye know him; for he dwelleth with you, and shall be in you. I will not leave you comfortless: I will come to you. (John 14:16-18)

Indeed, this is a very comforting passage of Scripture. Here, Jesus makes it very clear that those of us who have accepted him as our Lord and Savior, and have decided to follow him and his narrow way, have the Holy Spirit within and around us to encourage, strengthen, empower, and enable us to walk "...in the paths of righteousness for [Jesus'] name's sake" (Psalm 23:3).

Temptation, Deliverance, and Letting our Light Shine

As we Christians face temptation in this sinful and fallen world, and we consistently choose God's way instead of the ways of the world, we grow in sanctifying grace and holiness. The world takes notice of our holiness, and we witness to the reality of Christ and another kingdom. Jesus speaks of this in Matthew 5:14-16 where he proclaims that:

> Ye are the light of the world. A city that is set on a hill cannot be hid. Neither do men light a candle, and put it under a bushel, but on a candlestick; and it giveth light unto all that are in the house. Let your light so shine before men, that they may see your good works, and glorify your Father which is in heaven.

Indeed, we always have the option of obedience when faced with temptation, and, as we obey consistently and repetitively, we become holier. The world takes notice because holiness stands out in this sinful world within which we live and do ministry.

If you have any doubt about holiness standing out in our modern world and God being glorified in it, you may just look at the ministries of St. Teresa of Calcutta (Mother Teresa) and Rev. Dr. Billy Graham. They are examples of God's light shining, and God being glorified, through the consistent and perpetual obedience and dedication of one woman and one man who decided to live for, obey, love, and serve God. These two dedicated disciples of Jesus Christ rocked this fallen world for the King of kings and did much to expand his reign and rule on this earth as Jesus' kingdom came, here on earth, as it is in heaven, in their lives and ministries, to the glory of God the Father. (Matthew 5:16, 6:10) They accomplished great things for God, and their lights shined brightly, because they obeyed the words of Jesus, in Matthew 6:33 where he says: "...seek ye first the kingdom of God, and his righteousness; and all these things shall be added unto you."

Prayer, the Word, the Kingdom, and the Victory of Faith

God has provided all that we need in order for us to grow in holiness and for his kingdom to come here on earth, in our hearts and lives, as it is heaven. We Methodist Christians call these the "ordinary means of grace." They are the "ordinary" ways that God's grace and power come into the hearts and lives of those who trust in Jesus and strive to obey, follow, and serve him. The two "ordinary means of grace" that we always have with us no matter where we are are prayer and the Word. Indeed, we could find ourselves in a bad situation or place where we might not have a Bible nearby. This is why we need to study and memorize Scripture and hide it in our hearts. The Psalmist tells us to do this in Psalm 119:11 where he states: "Thy word have I hid in mine heart; that I might not sin against thee."

When we look at the temptation of Jesus in Matthew 4:1-11, we see that he stood on the Word of God, that he had hidden in his heart, each time he was tempted. Indeed, Jesus is God, the Second Person of the Holy Trinity, and he is the Word made flesh. (John 1:1,14) However, the account of his temptation in the wilderness in Matthew 4:1-11 is a story about the humanity of Christ. Our Christology in the Christian Church maintains that Jesus is 100% God and 100% man. He is not half God and half man, but he is 100% God and 100% man. The powerful story of his temptation in the wilderness is a story about the humanity of Christ, and it highlights the fact that he was a Jewish man who loved God and hid the Word of God in his heart.

As we look at the story of the temptation of Jesus in Matthew 4:1-11, we see that Jesus is very hungry and tired because he has been fasting in the wilderness for forty days and forty nights. The devil arrives to tempt him. This reminds us that the enemy will sometimes attack us, and tempt us, when we are physically or spiritually tired. We are also vulnerable when we are physically or spiritually hungry. We are to keep ourselves filled with prayer and the Word so that we don't become spiritually hungry. Jesus highlights this in the Fourth Beatitude where he states: "Blessed are they which do hunger and thirst after righteousness: for they shall be filled" (Matthew 5:6). By staying close to God through prayer, worship, and Bible study, our lives stay filled with the good things of God and our cups "…runneth over…" with God's grace and blessings. (Psalm 23:5)

In the first temptation, the enemy tempts Jesus to change the stones into bread. Jesus is very hungry, so this is a temptation in the physical realm. Although it would not necessarily be a sin for Jesus to change stones into bread to eat under normal circumstances, it would be a sin under these circumstances because it is the devil tempting him to do it.

Because of his love for his Father, and his desire to serve and do his Father's will, Jesus defeats this temptation by standing on the Word by stating: "...It is written, Man shall not live by bread alone, but by every word that proceedeth out of the mouth of God" (Matthew 4:4). Here, Jesus stands on Deuteronomy 8:3 which he had hidden in his heart, and he reminds us that the Bible is truly daily spiritual bread. Then, in the second temptation, the devil tempts Jesus to create a situation that will force the hand of God. The enemy tells Jesus to throw himself down from the pinnacle of the temple to test the promises of Psalm 91:9-12 which the devil paraphrases incorrectly. This is a temptation in the spiritual realm, and it is a temptation to doubt God's promises and have that doubt resolved by creating a situation within which God will have to act to keep his promises. Therefore, Jesus defeats the temptation by standing on Deuteronomy 6:16 and declares: "...It is written again, Thou shalt not tempt the Lord thy God" (Matthew 4:7). Then, in the third temptation, the enemy tempts Jesus in the material realm. The devil shows Jesus all the of the kingdoms of this world, and he promises Jesus that he can have them if Jesus will just fall down and worship him. (Matthew 4:8-9) Here, Jesus is tempted by the material things of the world, and he is tempted to put the things of this world, and the devil who controls them, before God.

This is a temptation that is very prevalent in the lives of Christian men and women living in our modern, post-Christian, society. The things of this world that glitter and shine, and the idols we put up on pedestals and bow down before never bring us joy, peace, or fulfillment. The devil never keeps his promises, and he is a liar and the father of lies. (John 8:44) The devil promises this and that, but he only delivers death, misery, hopelessness, and despair. This is what St. Paul speaks of in Romans 6:23 where he states: ",,, the wages of sin is death; but the gift of God is eternal life through Jesus Christ our Lord." When we refuse to create idols out of the things and celebrities in this world, and we refuse to love things that glitter and shine, we say "no" to the devil and "yes" to God. We keep God first in our lives, and we worship him, his Son, and the Holy Spirit only. Jesus Christ does keep his promises, and he never lies. Indeed, the Bible tells us in Numbers 23:19 "God is not a man, that he should lie;..." Jesus also tells us in John 14:6 that: "...I am the way, the truth, and the life: no man cometh unto the Father, but by me." Our Lord Jesus Christ not only tells truth, but he is the truth. He deserves first place in our lives, and he earned first place in our lives when he bled and died for us on that old rugged cross.

The New Covenant and the Kingdom of God

At the cross, when his blood was shed for sinners, he inaugurated the New Covenant and brought the kingdom of God near to us. Sin and death were destroyed, and our sins, which separated us from God and his kingdom, were atoned for once and for all. This is what Jeremiah prophesied about in Jeremiah 31:31-34 where he declares:

> Behold, the days come; saith the Lord, that I will make a new covenant with the house of Israel, and with the house of Judah: Not according to the covenant that I made with their fathers in the day that I took them by the hand to bring them out of the land of Egypt; which

my covenant they brake, although I was an husband unto them, saith the Lord: But this shall be the covenant that I will make with the house of Israel; After those days, saith the Lord, I will put my law in their inward parts, and write it in their hearts; and will be their God, and they shall be my people. And they shall teach no more every man his neighbor; and every man his brother; saying, Know the Lord; for they shall all know me, from the least of them unto the greatest of them, saith the Lord; for I will forgive their iniquity, and I will remember their sin no more.

The broken body and shed blood of Christ initiated the New Covenant in his blood, and men and women can now be truly reconciled to God and his kingdom forever by trusting in the atoning work of Christ at the cross. This is the Good News that is the Gospel. And, in his Advent, ministry, teachings, the example he set, his death, resurrection, and ascension, Jesus brought the kingdom, the power, and the glory of God here to earth and paved the way to heaven for all who trust in him. Since the blood of Christ was shed once-and-for-all, and it is a historical event that took place on a certain day in human history, it is something that God has "done" for us that cannot be "undone." At the cross, God has spoken and proclaimed that he loves us. And, he has not only spoken, but he has acted and proven his love for us by dying on the cross incarnate in the Jewish flesh of his Son our Lord, Jesus Christ. The crucifixion of Christ is God's great "yes" to the world, and it is the mighty act God has "done" for us. God has accomplished the inauguration of the New Covenant, and he has made salvation and reconciliation with God possible for every sinner, no matter how sinful, if they trust in Christ as their Lord and Savior. All of the glory for this goes to God because Jesus very clearly taught us in John 6:38 that: "...I came down from heaven, not to do mine own will, but the will of him that sent me." And, as Jesus looks to the cross, on the night before his crucifixion, he prays for his disciples, and us, and he begins the prayer with: "...Father, the hour is come; glorify thy Son, that thy Son also may glorify thee" (John 17:1). God is glorified in the mighty work and the kingdom of his Son our Lord, and all glory and honor is due him. Therefore, the kingdom that was established, on that beautiful yet wretched day at the cross, is without end and that is why we pray: "...thine is the kingdom, and the power, and the glory, for ever. Amen" (Matthew 6:13).

Chapter 7 – Matthew 6:14-15

14. For if ye forgive men their trespasses, your heavenly Father will also forgive you: 15. But if ye forgive not men their trespasses, neither will your heavenly Father forgive your trespasses.

Of all the theological themes expressed in the Lord's Prayer, Jesus only provides additional commentary on one and that is forgiveness. Forgiveness is a Biblical mandate, and it is one of the definitive teachings of Christ. As Christians, we are to show the love, mercy, and forgiveness to others that God has shown us. Along these lines, the apostle Paul states in Colossians 3:12-14:

> Put on therefore, as the elect of God, holy and beloved, bowels of mercies, kindness, humbleness of mind, meekness, longsuffering: Forbearing one another, and forgiving one another, if any man have a quarrel against any: even as Christ forgave you, so also do ye. And above all these things put on charity [love], which is the bond of perfectness.

Here, and in several other places in the New Testament, St. Paul highlights how love and forgiveness go hand in hand. If we refuse to love someone, we will not forgive them. And, if we refuse to forgive someone, we will not love them. God loves us because he has forgiven us by the way of the broken body and shed blood of his Son. Therefore, he expects us to forgive others so that we will be able to love them just as he forgave us so that he could love us. The apostle John sums it up beautifully by declaring:

> We love him, because he first loved us. If a man say, I love God, and hateth his brother, he is a liar: for he that loveth not his brother whom he hath seen, how can he love God whom he hath not seen? And this commandment have we from him, That he who loveth God love his brother also.
> (1 John 4:19-21)

Four Roadblocks to Forgiveness

There are many reasons that Christians sometimes refuse to forgive others. These are usually worldly reasons, and the Christian who opts to make excuses instead of forgiving is basically sinning and yielding to the flesh. As born-again and believing Christians, we are to obey the Commandments and teachings of Christ instead of yielding to our flesh and making excuses. Jesus plainly states: "If ye love me, keep my commandments" (John 14:15). If we truly love Jesus, and we want to obey him as our Lord, we will love others and loving others involves forgiving them when they sin against us. And, as we discussed earlier, we don't want to be lying to God when we pray the Lord's Prayer and ask God to forgive us as we forgive and are forgiving others. (Matthew 6:12) If we yield to the temptation of the flesh to refuse to forgive, and to hold a grudge against someone, we are not truly following Christ. Instead, we are following the devil because we are yielding to the temptation of the flesh to hold a grudge and refuse to forgive.

We rarely think of this as a temptation of the flesh, but it is. And, we sin if we yield to it and refuse to forgive others as God has forgiven us. In 1 Corinthians 13:7, St. Paul says love bears and endures and hopes and believes all things. Our love for one another should bear and endure our disagreements and differences of opinions. Also, Jesus tells us to go the second mile with those who compel us to go one mile. (Matthew 5:41) Sadly, we sometimes see where folks, claiming to be Christians following Christ, won't even go the first mile for others much less will they go the second mile. This should not be. If we claim to love, serve, and obey Jesus Christ, we should obey his Commandments that we love and forgive others as he has loved and forgiven us.

Roadblock to Forgiveness #1:
When There is No Repentance

Sometimes Christians incorrectly believe that they are only required to forgive others if they repent, apologize, admit they were wrong, and ask for forgiveness. When I hear this, I simply ask: "Do you want God to only forgive the sins you have acknowledged, repented of, apologized for, and asked God to forgive?" The answer is usually something like: "No, I want God to forgive all of my sins." So, if we want God to forgive all of our sins, not just the ones we have acknowledged, repented of, and asked for forgiveness for, why would we have the audacity to refuse forgiveness to someone who has not acknowledged, repented of, apologized for, and asked for forgiveness for their sin against us? This is hypocrisy if we refuse to show the grace and mercy to others that God has shown us. In John 15:10-12, Jesus explains by asserting:

If ye keep my commandments, ye shall abide in my love; even as I have kept my Father's commandments, and abide in his love. These things have I spoken unto you, that my joy might remain in you, and that your might be full. This is my commandment, That ye love one another, as I have loved you.

Roadblock to Forgiveness #2: The Gravity of the Offense

Sometimes the wrong done to the Christian is so hurtful and devastating that we fall into the worldly, "fleshly," trap of thinking that we don't have to forgive the sin because it is beyond forgiveness. If you are among those who are in this category, I have an exercise that will assist you in finding a way to forgive the person who hurt you or your loved one. If you are not a born-again believing Christian, this will be of very little help. However, if you are a saved and forgiven child of God, this will help you see the importance of forgiving all others, even those who have wronged us in the most hurtful and painful ways. Just close your eyes and think and remember the worst sin you ever committed. In other words, think and remember the worst thing you have ever done. Now, with your eyes still closed, remember a fairly "minor" sin that you have committed. Now, I ask you, which one do you think would jeopardize your salvation if it were not under the blood of Jesus? Would it be the worst sin you have ever committed or the sin that you think is a fairly "minor" sin? The answer is that either one of these sins, the worst sin you have ever committed and the relatively "minor" sin, would separate you from God for all of eternity if it were not atoned for and covered by the broken body and shed blood of Jesus on the cross.

Therefore, since God doesn't pick and choose which sins we are forgiven of, we should not pick and choose which sins we forgive others for. God justifies us and declares us "not guilty" when we trust in Christ as Savior and begin serving and obeying him as Lord. We Methodist Christians call this justifying grace, and it is the grace that we enter into when we trust in Christ, and his atoning work at the cross, and we experience the New Birth and the Holy Spirit enters into our hearts and lives. Now that the Holy Spirit is with us, we can begin our journey in sanctifying grace, and we grow holier in heart and life everyday as we consistently choose the narrow way of Jesus which leads to abundant and eternal life. (Romans 5:1, Matthew 7:13-14, and John 10:10)

Roadblock to Forgiveness #3: When We Just Don't Like the Person Who Sinned Against Us

Now, this one is very prevalent in our worldly culture and even in the contemporary church. We sometimes fall into that worldly way of thinking that forgiveness is one of those "nice" things we do primarily for our friends and members of our families. However, when you accepted Jesus as Savior, you also accepted him as Lord, and he has certain expectations of you as a Christian disciple. His Commandments are not complicated, and, if our hearts and minds are in the right place, his Commandments are not too difficult. They can be summed up quite succinctly. Jesus has forgiven you of all your sins, so he expects you to forgive all the sins that are committed against you. Jesus loves you regardless of all the sins you have committed in your lifetime, so he expects you to love all others.

Quite frankly, we Christians are simply not allowed to decide we "don't like" someone. If you want to be able to "not like" some people, you may be a good candidate for some other religion. Christianity requires that you love God and all others and that you forgive all sins committed against you just as God has forgiven all of your sins. If you are truly born-again, and the Holy Spirit is active in your heart and life, you will develop a strong recognition of the great amount of forgiveness you have received from God. And, you will begin to understand the great hypocrisy that is evident when a professing Christian withholds forgiveness after having received so much forgiveness from God.

Indeed, those who have been forgiven much love Jesus very much, and this is evident in the story of the woman who washed Jesus feet with her tears, dried them with her hair, and anointed him with oil. She loved Jesus much because she had been forgiven much. (Luke 7:36-50) Jesus speaks of her and says: "...I say unto thee, Her sins, which are many, are forgiven; for she loved much: but to whom little is forgiven, the same loveth little" (Luke 7:47). Every truly saved, born-again, and believing Christian has been forgiven very much, so let us not demonstrate the hypocrisy, and lack of love for and obedience to Jesus, that is involved when we don't forgive someone, simply because we have decided that we "don't like" him or her. If we truly love Jesus, and appreciate what he did for us at the cross, and are striving to follow and obey him as our Lord, we will love all others, and we will forgive all others. Jesus makes this very clear in John 14:15 where he states: "If ye love me, keep my commandments."

Roadblock to Forgiveness #4: Selfishness, Limiting Forgiveness, and Giving Into the Fleshly Desire to Hold a Grudge

Unfortunately, many Christians stand before the cross in church on Sunday and affirm that they believe in Jesus Christ as they recite the Apostles' Creed; however, many of them frequently do not truly follow him when it comes to forgiving someone or loving enemies. When we decide to be serious about following Christ, and being his disciples, we will learn to forgive, and we will learn to love our enemies. The joy and peace that comes from truly following Jesus are to be found in a profound obedience based on love and appreciation for our Lord and all that he accomplished for us at the cross.

Our love for Jesus, and our thankfulness to him, doesn't make forgiving others and loving enemies easy, but it does equip and empower to do so. We must remember that our Christian walk is between us and our Lord and not us and the whole world. We obey the more difficult teachings of Jesus because we love him, and we want to be near him. We obey him because we want him to be proud of us, and we want to be his sheep. We want to be counted among the sheep Jesus speaks of in John 10:27-29 where he says:

> My sheep hear my voice, and I know them, and they follow me. And I give unto them eternal life; and they shall never perish, neither shall any man pluck them out of my hand. My Father which gave them me, is greater than all; and no man is able to pluck them out of my Father's hand.

We all have two voices that we hear and can follow. One is the voice of the world and our potentially sinful selves, and the other is the voice of our Good Shepherd who speaks to us through the presence of the Holy Spirit. We grow in holiness and sanctifying grace as we consistently obey the voice of the Lord and say "no" to our "fleshly" desires which arise from our rebellious and potentially sinful fallen natures. Each day, we face the same decision that Joshua speaks of in Joshua 24:15 as he tells the Israelites:

> And if it seem evil unto you to serve the Lord, choose you this day whom ye will serve; whether the gods which your fathers served that were on the other side of the flood, or the gods of the Amorites, in whose land ye dwell; but as for me and my house, we will serve the Lord.

As we grow in holiness and sanctifying grace, we will need to be aware of our tendency to be selfish. We live in a world where selfishness is not only accepted, but it is encouraged and rewarded. Christ teaches us to live our lives for God and others and not for ourselves. This continues to be a radical way to live, and it continues to be anti-intuitive and counter-cultural. We Christians are Christocentric, Christ-centered, people, and we are not egocentric, self-centered, people. We realize that life is not about me, myself, and I, but it is about

Jesus Christ our Lord and the kingdom of God. We find true meaning and purpose in our lives when we deny ourselves and take up our crosses and follow Christ. In Matthew 16:24-25, Jesus explains by asserting:

> ...If any man will come after me, let him deny himself, and take up his cross, and follow me. For whosoever will save his life shall lose it: and whosoever will lose his life for my sake shall find it.

Our lives have meaning and purpose as we deny ourselves, and our flesh, and take up our crosses and follow Jesus. Forgiveness is one of those areas where self, and selfishness, can get in the way of us doing what God calls us to do. We don't want to let sin, selfishness, or this worldly culture we live in to get in the way of our obedience to Christ and his teachings.

Jesus not only taught us how to live for and serve others, but he also showed us how to live for and serve others in his life, ministry, death, and resurrection. Anyone can say that they "deny" themselves, and talk is cheap. Words are indeed important, and they have their place. However, actions speak louder than words. Jesus demonstrated that he loved us by humbling himself and giving himself for us on the cross. We, as his disciples, are to follow his example of humility and sacrifice and be willing to love, and lay down our lives, for others as Christ laid down his life for us, to the glory of God. Jesus makes this clear in John 15:13 where he declares: "Greater love hath no man than this, that a man lay down his life for his friends."

St. Teresa of Calcutta (Mother Teresa) laid down her life for the hungry, sickly, suffering, and forgotten children, women, and men of Calcutta, India. The entire world, not just Roman Catholic Christians, agree that she is literally a saint, an angel of God, who made God's kingdom come, and made God's will be done, on earth, in the slums of Calcutta, as it is in heaven. The apostle Paul sums up beautifully how Jesus humbled himself, and gave himself for us, in Philippians 2:5-8 where he states:

> Let this mind be in you, which was also in Christ Jesus: Who, being in the form of God, thought it not robbery to be equal with God: But made himself of no reputation, and took

upon him the form of a servant, and was made in the likeness of men: And being found in fashion as a man, he humbled himself, and became obedient unto death, even the death of the cross.

The glory of the Christian life is found in denying self and allowing the teachings of Christ to be lived out in practical ways in our lives. Then, we live selflessly instead of selfishly, and we experience the abundant life that Jesus said he came to give us. (John 10:10) We no longer live to see how much we can gain or how much we can take, but we live to see how much we can give and how much we can share with others. We do this because our minds have been "renewed," and we now think like God thinks. And, we do like God does. This is what St. Teresa of Calcutta (Mother Teresa) did, and this is what true holiness is all about. It is about: "Thy kingdom come, Thy will be done in earth, as it is in heaven" (Matthew 6:9). And, it is about: "Be ye therefore perfect, even as your Father which is in heaven is perfect" (Matthew 5:48).

Chapter 8 – Conclusion

In our study of the Lord's Prayer, we are reminded of many of the foundational truths about life. We are also reminded of the many foundational truths about Christian discipleship. People in a free society basically do what they want to do, and they, for the most part, go where they want to go. Freedom is one of the greatest blessings we have in America, and Christians in many parts of the world are free to practice Christianity and to serve Christ. We should strive to take full advantage of this great freedom that so many fought and died to secure and defend for us. We are forever thankful to our Veterans for their sacrifice, courage, and service, and we thank God that we are free in our great country, The United States of America, to learn and live the teachings of our Lord and Savior, Jesus Christ. We will never forget the women and men of the Armed Forces who gave their lives, limbs, and liberty so that we could be free.

We are also spiritually free to obey the teachings of Christ and to grow in holiness. Because Christ has fulfilled the law by dying as a once-and-for-all perfect Sacrifice on the cross, we no longer have to go out and buy animals for the priest to use as offerings for us to atone for our sins. Christ has atoned for our sins once-and-for-all at the cross.

Living Sacrifices

Since our sins have been atoned for by Christ at the cross, we are no longer slaves to sin, but we are slaves to righteousness. The apostle Paul explains in Romans 6:16-18 where he states:

> Know ye not that to whom ye yield yourselves servants to obey; his servants ye are to whom ye obey;, whether of sin unto death, or of obedience unto righteousness? But God be thanked that ye were the servants of sin, but ye have obeyed from the heart that form of doctrine which was delivered you. Being then made free from sin, ye became the servants of righteousness.

The freedom we enjoy as Christian disciples is to be enjoyed by living out the Great Commandments of Christ which are that we love God and each other. As we do this day in and day out, we are strengthened in righteousness, and we grow in sanctifying grace. Occasionally, we may be tempted to hold a grudge, to withhold forgiveness, and to join in with the popular group who excludes and criticizes others. However, we don't have to fall into this trap. We can choose righteousness instead, and we are given the opportunity to choose righteousness every time. Let us make the right choices so that we will continue growing in holiness to the glory of God,

In Romans 12:1-2, St. Paul states:

> I beseech you therefore, brethren, by the mercies of God, that ye present your bodies a living sacrifice, holy, acceptable unto God, which is your reasonable service. And be not conformed to this world: but be ye transformed by the renewing of your mind, that ye may prove what is that good, and acceptable, and perfect, will of God.

Here, Paul helps us to understand the importance of refusing the ways of the world while allowing our minds to be changed to God's perspective, The renewing of the mind involves seeing things the way God sees them. It is getting our thoughts and perspectives in line with God's thoughts and perspectives. This is what true holiness is. When we agree with God that sin is sin, and good works are good works, we are now living as living sacrifices to God to his glory and for the expansion of his kingdom.

The Enemy Named Selfishness

Selfishness tempts us to make our own rules concerning forgiveness, enemy love, and the other more challenging aspects of Christian discipleship. Sometimes we obey Christ, and we do what he commands, but we impose limits on forgiveness or leave certain types of sinners and criminals out when it comes to Christian ministry, compassion, forgiveness, and love. When this temptation arises, we will do well to remember that we are all "felons" in the eyes of our perfectly sinless and holy God. We would all be sentenced to death and eternal separation from God if it weren't for the broken body and shed blood of Jesus broken and poured out for us at the cross. From the meanest of murderers to the teenager stealing a bicycle from his neighbor's garage, we "...all have sinned, and come short of the glory of God..." (Romans 3:23). Therefore, we are to forgive others as God has forgiven us, and we are to love others as God has loved us.

Selfishness and Limiting Forgiveness

Because we live in this worldly culture, and we live in these "fleshly" bodies, we need to be aware of our sinful tendencies when it comes to the more challenging aspects of Christian discipleship. We will want to omit and exclude certain persons from receiving our forgiveness based on our "sinful" and "fleshly" point of view. We all have those who we sometimes consider or would prefer for them to be excluded from God's love and forgiveness. And, we also like to put human limits on the things of the kingdom of God when the kingdom of God is limitless in love and forgiveness. If we are honest with ourselves, we are disturbed by the reality that: "...whosoever shall call upon the name of the Lord shall be saved" (Romans 10:13). However, this is the reality of the unlimited grace and love of almighty God. He loves and forgives every "sinner" who accepts Jesus as Savior, and trusts in his broken body and shed blood at the cross as the only atonement for his or her sins, and repents and begins following and obeying Jesus as Lord. Jesus makes it very clear that this salvation is available to "whosoever," in that immortal verse of Scripture which has brought hope and salvation to great multitudes of sinners, in John 3:16 where he proclaims:

> For God so loved the world, that he gave his only begotten Son, that whosoever believeth in him should not perish, but have everlasting life.

God loves the whole "world," and this includes everyone. No one, no matter how evil and wicked, is outside of God's love. God loves everyone, and he forgives every sin, minor and major sins, of everyone who puts their trust in Christ who is "...the Lamb of God, which taketh away the sin of the world" (John 1:29).

The idea that certain persons can be excluded when it comes to forgiveness or we only have to forgive persons a limited number of times has been around a long time. Actually, Peter asks Jesus about this in Matthew 18:21-22 where we read:

> Then came Peter to him, and said, Lord how oft shall my brother sin against me, and I forgive him? till seven times? Jesus saith unto him, I say not unto thee, Until seven times; but, Until seventy times seven.

We are not to limit the number of times we forgive someone. He tells Peter not only is he to forgive seven times, but he is to forgive seventy times seven times which is four hundred and ninety times. Now, unless we have a spreadsheet on our smart phone or laptop, and we have diligently entered each person we have forgiven, and each time we have forgiven them, we are simply not going to know when we get to the four hundred and ninety-first offense. Therefore, Jesus is teaching us not to limit how many times we forgive. We are to forgive others however many times they sin against us just as God forgives every sin we commit against him. We are to forgive as God has forgiven us, and we are to love as God has loved us. God's love and forgiveness for us is unlimited, and our love and forgiveness of others should be unlimited as well. This is what St. Paul speaks of in 1 Corinthians 13:5-7 where he states that love:

> Doth not behave itself unseemly, seeketh not her own, is not easily provoked, thinketh no evil; Rejoiceth not in iniquity, but rejoiceth in the truth; Beareth all things, believeth all things, hopeth all things, endureth all things.

Since we frequently read 1 Corinthians 13 at weddings, we are sometimes tempted to think that we are only required to love our spouses with this "love" that bears and endures all things. However, Paul says nothing about this being applied only to husband and wife.

He is describing the kind of love that God has for us. It is the kind of love that brings a King to a cross. It is the kind of love that is crowned with a crown of thorns. It is the kind of love that bleeds and dies as his mother looks on and cries. It is the kind of love that falls beneath the weight of the cross, and then thinks of you missing out on salvation, and summons the strength and courage to pick the cross back up and continue down the Via Delarosa. It is the kind of love that looks to heaven in victory and proclaims: "...'It is finished'..." (John 19:30). It is the kind of love that looks to a sinner, who has allowed sin to ruin his life but in his last moments decides to trust in Christ, and says: "...'Verily I say unto thee, to day shalt thou be with me in paradise.'" (Luke 23:43) This is how much God loves us, and this is how much God calls, equips, and empowers us to love others. We must not give in to our sinful and worldly temptation to limit forgiveness or to consider certain "sinners" outside the arena of forgiveness. God loves and forgives all sinners who trust in Christ as Lord and Savior, and he expects you and me to do the same.

The question we find ourselves asking at the conclusion of our study of the Lord's Prayer is do we want these petitions granted? Do we truly want the kingdom of God to come into our hearts, homes, lives, and communities? Do we truly want God's will to be done in our hearts, homes, lives, and communities? If we pray the Lord's Prayer in church every Sunday, and we pray it at other times and events in our lives, we need to be very aware of what we are asking of God and what we are telling God in prayer. We must be willing to hold ourselves accountable to the words we pray, and we must be willing to make the sacrifices that are necessary in order to shape our hearts and lives in a way that God can pour out his blessings upon us. This happens as we consistently say "no" to self and say "yes" to God, and we have the Word of God to guide us in our journey. The journey to holiness is a glorious adventure, and it is an adventure experienced as we walk hand in hand with our Lord and Savior, Jesus Christ.

The enemy we have most to fear is self. We are the ones who have it within us to disobey and say "no" to God. We must be aware of this, and we must be willing to put self in its place when it attempts to rise within us. Many have likened it to having a good angel on one shoulder and a bad angel on the other. One suggests that we take the way of holiness and obedience, and the other suggests that we take the way of sin and disobedience. The bad angel is usually made up in part of self and the good angel is also made up of self. If we keep Jesus first in our lives, and we stay in his Word, he will show us the right way to go in all circumstances. He will lead us "...in the paths of righteousness for his name's sake" (Psalm 23:3). And, he will also empower and equip us to live as we pray as we continue praying together: "Thy kingdom come. Thy will be done in earth, as it is in heaven" (Matthew 6:10).

Made in the USA
Columbia, SC
29 September 2017